SWATI SENGUPTA is an author and journalist. Her books include *Out of War* (Speaking Tiger Books, 2016), *Guns on My Red Earth* (Rupa, 2013), *Half the Field Is Mine* (Scholastic, 2014), *The Talking Bird* (Tulika Books, 2014) and *A Tea Garden Party* (Pratham Books, 2021). She translated *Murder In The City* by Supratim Sarkar (Speaking Tiger Books, 2018) from Bengali to English. Swati runs a workshop series on gender for young adults. She studied English at Jadavpur University and lives in Kolkata.

Also in the series by Swati Sengupta:

Milkha Singh: The Runner Who Could Fly

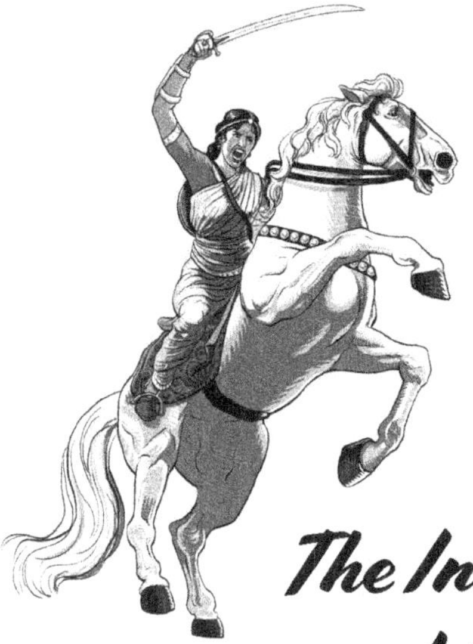

The Incredible Life of
Jhalkari Bai
The Braveheart Warrior

Swati Sengupta

Illustrations by Devashish Verma

An Imprint of Speaking Tiger Books

TALKING CUB

Published by Speaking Tiger Books LLP
125A, Ground Floor, Shahpur Jat,
Near Asiad Village, New Delhi 110 049

First published in paperback in Talking Cub
by Speaking Tiger Books in 2022

Text copyright © Swati Sengupta 2022

Illustration copyright © Speaking Tiger Books 2022

ISBN: 978-93-5447-377-7

eISBN: 978-93-5447-375-3

10 9 8 7 6 5 4 3 2 1

No part of this publication may be reproduced, transmitted, or stored in a retrieval system, in any form or by any means, electronic, mechanical, photocopying, recording or otherwise, without the prior permission of the publisher.

This book is sold subject to the condition that it shall not, by way of trade or otherwise, be lent, resold, hired out, or otherwise circulated, without the publisher's prior consent, in any form of binding or cover other than that in which it is published.

To Subhadra Sen Gupta,
for igniting a passion for history in young readers.
And all the other SSGs I know.

Chapter One

She loved exploring the unknown. Sometimes, she would walk right up to the rugged hilltop to watch the sun, like a huge ball of fire, bob up in the sky, filling the land with wondrous colours.

Sometimes, she would explore the depths of the forest when she went to collect wood for the kitchen fire. Today, Jhalri had ventured deep into the forest. She slashed a few dried branches with the axe she was carrying. When there were enough twigs and branches, she tied them with a rope. It was a heavy bunch, enough to last for a few days. The teenage Jhalri tottered under its weight, but quickly regained her balance. Her father, Sadova Singh, had taught her to be strong.

He always encouraged her to run, jump and do other physical activities that would help build a strong body. A strong body gives you the confidence to have a strong mind, he said.

Jhalri could walk for hours under the hot sun of Bhojla and not get tired. In fact, she enjoyed the heat. She loved the winter chill just as much. Her father would set fire to dry leaves and twigs, which would burn all evening to keep them warm.

Their village, Bhojla, was 10 kilometres from Jhansi. The king and the queen lived in Jhansi, where, she had heard, there was an enormous fort that King Virsingha had built many years ago. Jhalri often thought about Jhansi, the king, queen, the palace and how brave the soldiers in their army must be. Now, as she walked through the forest, her mind drifted once more to Jhansi and its illustrious kings who had ruled over this land for so many years. Secretly, Jhalri wanted to be a soldier and fight in the army.

She took a long, dry branch and imagined it to be a sword. She whipped the branch through the air and thought how she would plunge the sword into the enemy's chest. In her mind's eye, she could see the soldier drop dead in a single blow. She pulled out the sword blade and lifted it up in the air, victorious. She imagined thousands of people applauding her feat.

The silence of the forest was enchanting. This was her own world which *she* ruled. She picked up the bunch of twigs and branches on her head once more. She needed to head home now and help her father with the cooking. But right then, something sent a cold shiver down her spine!

Her eyes met another pair of eyes from behind the bushes, just a few feet away. Those were *not* human eyes.

Jhalri knew that the best way to defend herself from wild animals was to remain still. So she pretended to be a statue. But the screams of a goat at a distance suddenly alarmed her and she fell on the ground with her bundle of firewood. The tiger, its eyes glowing now, got alarmed too. It began to growl under its breath, its piercing eyes looking straight at Jhalri.

Tigers would not attack humans unless they had some bitter experience with them in the past.

Perhaps that's why it was so angry? Perhaps it was old and hurt and hadn't got enough to eat for the past few days? For whatever reason, the huge animal lunged at Jhalri now.

Swiftly, the young girl reached for the axe tied to her waist. She aimed it at the attacking tiger from a distance. The axe missed and flew through the air in a curve and got stuck in a tree trunk.

She was now totally unarmed, her only weapon, her strength. She jumped into the air and caught hold of the tiger's forelimbs with her two hands and walloped the animal with one powerful blow. It was a huge tiger, perhaps several times heavier than she was. It fell back on the ground, startled and hurt. But then it quickly steadied itself and gave out a roar that pierced the stillness of the forest.

Bruised and angry, it swiped at Jhalri's face with its forelimb. She swiftly ducked. Though it missed her face, the tiger's claws slashed her flesh and lacerated her arm. Blood gushed out. The pain made her head spin. She was now wrestling on the ground with the tiger. The animal was strong and powerful, and so was Jhalri.

A wounded girl can be just as dangerous as an injured tiger. Jhalri stood up and taking advantage of the tiger having fallen down, she used both her hands to grab the tiger's jaws, and pulled them apart. The animal gave out an agonizing cry. Everything stood still for a few brief moments. Jhalri readied herself to retaliate if the tiger pounced on her again. But it didn't move. The tiger was dead.

Jhalri sat down, relieved. A strange sorrow engulfed her. She had not wanted to kill the tiger, but she was helpless, for it had attacked her and would have killed her. A faint smile played on her lips as she suddenly became aware of her enormous power.

She tore an end of her flowing lehenga and tied her wound to stop the flow of blood. Then she picked up her bundle of sticks and branches, pulled out the axe from the tree trunk with some effort, and headed home. The tiger lay dead in a pool of blood in the middle of the forest.

This is the story of Jhalkari Bai, whose parents fondly called her Jhalri or Chaloria. The fearless Jhalkari Bai's name may not be known as widely as that of Rani Laxmibai of Jhansi, but her story of bravery, of fighting the British alongside the queen of Jhansi, is no less fascinating.

Her remarkable courage and the way she fought is etched in the minds of the people of Bundelkhand. Songs, poetry, plays and stories of Jhalkari Bai, or Jhalkari Bai Kori, tell inspiring tales not only of the first war of Independence of

1857 and her bravery, but also of the struggles of a Dalit woman.

In central India lies the rugged terrain of Bundelkhand, which means the domain of the Bundelas. The Bundelas, over many generations, created kingdoms in this area.

One of these kingdoms was Jhansi, located between the rivers Betwa and Pahuj. Jhansi attracted people from surrounding areas to settle there for their livelihood. It welcomed all, irrespective of their caste, creed, religion and other differences. There were Brahmans, Rajputs, Bundelas, Chamars, Koris or Kolis, Lodhis, Kachhis, Kurmis and so on. Owners of horses and elephants also reached Jhansi, and it became a centre of trade for these animals. There was cloth-weaving, agriculture, carpet making, pottery and various kinds of work that people depended on for their livelihood.

Jhansi prospered during the reign of the Chandela Rajputs. After the Chandelas, Jhansi was ruled by several kings, till it came under the control of the Mughals. At that time, Orchha was the capital of Bundelkhand.

During the 17th century, Virsingha was on the Bundela throne and he backed the rebel Mughal prince Salim (later Jahangir) against his father, Akbar. Akbar sent his men after Virsingha but was not able to defeat him. At a battle along the border of Orchha, Virsingha won. Subsequently, he announced himself the ruler of the entire region of Orchha and built three forts at Datia,

Dhamauni and Jhansi. The Jhansi fort was constructed in 1613.

Several decades later, Aurangzeb was on the Mughal throne and the Bundelkhand region was ruled by Maharaja Chattrasal. The maharaja divided his kingdom into three parts, and Jhansi, along with Kalpi, Etah, Hridaynagar and Jalaun, were given to Peshwa Bajirao I along with other adjoining areas.

Bajirao divided his kingdom into various parts but died prematurely. Naroshankar Motiwale was put in charge of Jhansi and he established a city that gradually grew around the fort.

In 1770, Peshwa Madhavrao I appointed Raghunath Hari Newalkar as subedar of Jhansi.

Under Raghunath Hari Newalkar, Jhansi flourished greatly for the next two decades.

It became a centre of trade and crafts. There was a library with Sanskrit books, and scholarly research was done. He also built the Mahalakshmi Temple and the Raghunath Temple. He constructed the beautiful Rani Mahal in the city.

Raghunath Hari Newalkar retired from his post in 1794. His younger brother Shivrao Bhau took over as subedar of Jhansi after that. In 1804, Shivrao Bhau signed a pact with the East India Company, which had several conditions. The East India Company, after some changes made in the agreement in 1806, granted Shivrao Bhau and his heirs the right to rule over Jhansi. Shivrao Bhau died in 1816.

In 1817, Peshwa Bajirao II let the East India Company have full authority over Bundelkhand.

The East India Company also accepted Ramchandra Rao as the successor of Shivrao Bhau. In 1821, when Ramchandra Rao became old enough to take charge, he helped the British by giving them money, weapons and soldiers. With such close ties, the British soon granted Ramchandra Rao the title of 'Raja' or king. The then Governor-General of India, William Bentinck, visited Jhansi on 9 December 1832. At a grand ceremony, he conferred the title on Ramchandra Rao.

Meanwhile however, the Rajput principalities of Orchha and Datia were envious of the progress made by the Maratha kingdom of Jhansi. They created trouble in some areas. The Rajput leaders then incited and provoked a struggle over land rights and a rebellion soon formed. Ramchandra

Rao's army was defeated. The entire principality was taken from Ramchandra Rao, except for Mauranipur and Jhansi.

But by then, Jhansi's coffers had been drained out. Ramchandra Rao mortgaged his kingdom and took a loan from the British. When Ramchandra Rao died, Raghunath Rao, Shivraj Bhau's son from a second marriage, was chosen king, in 1835. But he died, after suffering from leprosy, three years later and Gangadhar Rao, Shivrao Bhau's son, laid claim to the throne and the East India Company chose him.

Jhansi's coffers were almost empty, and the East India Company did not allow Gangadhar Rao to rule Jhansi independently. Instead, they gave him an allowance. However, Gangadhar Rao turned out to be a sincere administrator.

He eventually got married to a girl named Manikarnika, the daughter of Bhagirathibai and Moropant Tambe. Manikarnika was re-named Laxmibai after her marriage to Gangadhar Rao. He was nearly thirty years old, and Laxmibai was only eight years old at the time of their marriage.

Meanwhile, on 22 November 1830, in a village called Bhojla, 10 kilometres from Jhansi, a girl was born to Sadova Singh and Jamuna Devi. Her mother died when Jhalri was a little girl. The child grew up in an ordinary family, far from the happenings of Jhansi, which was preoccupied with the saga of princes and princesses, kings, queens, battles and administration. When she grew up, she was married to Puran Kori. Koris are Dalits whose traditional occupation was weaving and agriculture.

The story of Jhalkari Bai, a girl growing up in a small corner of Bundelkhand, is strangely intertwined with that of Laxmibai—and the politics and history of the rulers of this region.

> Jhalkari Bai's story is usually mentioned as a footnote in history books. The details of her life can, instead, be found in the melas of Bhojla, the village where she was born. It is to be found in songs and plays and oral histories. It can be found in the thin booklets and pamphlets that are sold in village fairs or in small bookstalls by the side of roads. They were not written by renowned historians but by unknown people you've never heard about. However, that does not make the story of Jhalkari Bai any less important than that of many more well-known freedom fighters. Why are these books available in abundance while official textbooks make so little mention of her?

Is it because Jhalkari was not born a princess, but was a girl from a so-called lower caste? And is it because history books usually tell the accounts of those who are powerful?

Chapter Two

After the encounter with the tiger in the forest, when Jhalri returned home, her father was shell-shocked to see her state. Her clothes were soaked in blood and sweat, her lehenga was torn and a piece of cloth was tied to her arm. Blood oozed from the wound.

'What happened, Jhalri?' he almost screamed.

'Nothing father, it was a tiger,' she replied.

'A what...? A what...?' her father stuttered. He could not believe his ears.

'A tiger... it was going to attack me, so I had to

kill it... I didn't mean to kill a poor animal, but it attacked me in the forest when I went to fetch wood for the fire,' Jhalri explained.

Sadova Singh's heart sank. His only child had just had a close shave! The poor child's mother was long dead, and Sadova Singh guarded his daughter with his life. How did he not think of the dangers in the forest before sending her there!

He helped Jhalkari wash her wounds and took her to a neighbourhood physician. Then he cooked while Jhalkari rested on the bed. Sadova Singh was suddenly aware of his daughter's enormous strength.

Jhalkari was not interested in cooking and cleaning, stitching or working in the fields. Though she was an obedient girl and did everything she was asked to do to help him, what she really enjoyed was running and playing outside. She had good stamina and strength. When the soldiers from the Jhansi army passed by their village, she watched them in fascination. When she was a little girl, Jhalri had told Sadova Singh that she wanted to own a horse. She would ride the horse straight to the mountaintop, travel through forests, cross rivers and fight wars, she told him.

'That's not for women, my dear baby girl,' her father, and her mother Jamuna Devi, told her. But secretly, both parents dreamed that Jhalkari would grow up and ride on horseback, excel in stick fighting and do whatever else she wanted to. They wanted their child to be able to fulfil her every dream. It was tough being poor and being a woman, but as parents they too were happy to dream Jhalkari's dreams.

As Sadova Singh sat there cooking, he remembered his conversations with his wife. He wanted Jhalkari to realize her dreams. So, to begin with, he decided to teach her stick fighting. That would encourage her and make her strong and confident. She was already physically powerful. Good training would make her invincible.

Several months had passed since Jhalkari had killed the tiger. Stories of her bravery had spread far and wide. Some people found it hard to believe that she had actually killed a tiger.

Every evening, after dinner, when she lay on

her cot, Jhalkari would conjure up various images of herself. She saw herself riding a horse—a huge powerful brown one. She could see herself dressed like a Pathan, her head covered with a turban, brandishing a sword. Jhalkari knew she would make a brave warrior. But would she ever be able to fight a 'real' war?

One evening, as she lay dreaming, she heard some muffled voices at a distance. The voices, though coming from quite far, appeared to be of people in panic. She tiptoed out, careful not to wake her father, carrying the stick she used for their stick fighting sessions. Everything was still. Their neighbours seemed to have gone off to sleep.

Up ahead, she spotted something outside a house, a torch with fire burning at one end had been stuck on the ground. As she went further, she heard threatening voices followed by muffled pleadings. Jhalkari peeped through a window of the house and her eyes popped out in disbelief! Inside were three men looting money, and her neighbours had been tied up with ropes, their mouths gagged with cloth. The dacoits were filling sacks with coins and jewellery, rice and dal.

Jhalkari stepped into the house with a sudden swiftness that took the dacoits by surprise. She used her stick, moving it deftly through the air, and injured all three dacoits within a few minutes. Their screams, followed by Jhalkari's threats, woke up all the neighbours who now came rushing in. Sensing trouble, the dacoits decided to run for cover. They left the coins, jewellery and foodgrains behind.

Jhalkari's father had rushed out too, and found that his daughter had trounced three dacoits within minutes! That night, Sadova Singh was yet again filled with pride and worry. He understood how strong and powerful Jhalkari was, but feared that her hopes to do something outstanding were doomed to be dashed. He calmed himself slowly and as he drifted off to sleep, there was a wonderful feeling that despite the odds, his daughter would make him proud one day.

Chapter Three

The story of Jhalkari's encounter with the tiger and the way she sent the dacoits running had spread far and wide. Everyone in Bhojla now knew of the strongest girl in their village. They were proud of her and were also afraid of her.

Not only in Bhojla, even the people of Jhansi had come to know about this brave girl. One such person was Puran Kori, a soldier in Jhansi. Puran, an attractive young man, served in the army of Jhansi. He was very impressed by Jhalkari's story. 'This is the kind of woman that

I would like to marry,' he thought to himself. He kept wondering how his dreams would be realized unless he actually told someone about it. Finally, Puran told his mother. 'I would like to marry a brave woman like Jhalkari.'

Puran's mother knew that her son was serious. She approached Jhalkari's father and the two families discussed their marriage. Soon, Puran Kori and Jhalkari Bai's wedding took place in a simple, traditional ceremony. Jhalkari was happy that she was chosen not for her beauty but for her courage.

After they got married, Puran taught her wrestling, horse riding and shooting. They were happy together because they had so many common interests. He enjoyed horse riding and she loved it too. They would mark trees, and from a distance they would aim arrows at the target they set. They made these events competitive to see who could hit arrows closest to the target, or run faster. Sometimes Puran won and sometimes Jhalkari beat him. How they laughed!

On days Puran didn't have much work, he and Jhalkari would set off on horses for distant hills. Jhalkari didn't know much of Jhansi, and she was amazed to see its beauty—undulating hills, dense forests, settlements here and there, the paved and cobbled roads, the river Betwa flowing quietly. The rugged terrain was Jhansi's true beauty. Peace and prosperity prevailed here. It was a new experience for her, visiting the temples, sitting by the side of lakes, riding horses, all with Puran by her side.

The city of Jhansi was encircled by walls. There were ten gates that allowed people to enter and exit. The royal palace was beautiful. There was a lake on one side of the city and a sprawling field near the palace where the soldiers could practise their drills and conduct their training. Puran practised here regularly with others in the Jhansi army.

Jhalkari would often walk around the city with Puran and gape at the beautiful palace and the Jhansi fort wondering if she could ever step into those enormous structures some day. Sometimes, Puran would tell Jhalkari stories of the palace and of the queen. The royal palace had beautiful lawns and fountains, its sprawling halls and rooms had soft carpets that caressed the feet of whoever stood on them. The women in the palace wore beautiful Chanderi sarees and brocade blouses, and jewellery of gold and silver. Even the women who worked for the queen wore beautiful sarees and jewellery and had flowers in their hair.

Jhalkari, however, wasn't attracted to gold and silver, nor did she crave for beautiful sarees. She was drawn to the fort. It was built over a huge area of 15 acres. When she looked at the fort and the palace, she wondered about the horses, the soldiers, the guards and the big cannons in there. But it would be difficult, perhaps impossible, for her to ever set foot in the palace and the fort. After all, almost every marker was against her. She was a woman, poor, and a Dalit.

But life was to change for Jhalkari soon, and

her name would be remembered by every person in Jhansi, Bhojla and beyond.

On 21 November 1853, Gangadhar Rao, the ruler of Jhansi, died at the age of forty. His wife Laxmibai, was eighteen years old then. They had a child, Damodar, but he had died when he was only three months old. A day before his death, Gangadhar Rao adopted five-year-old Ananda and his name was changed to Damodar Gangadhar Rao. He was related to the king as a grandson.

The British were on good terms with Gangadhar Rao, and under him Jhansi had become prosperous after a long time. After his death, the queen wrote a letter to Governor-

General Dalhousie, informing him about the adoption and sought its recognition. Around this time, the British had introduced a policy called the Doctrine of Lapse. According to this policy, princely states were 'de-recognized' or abolished and taken over by the British if the ruler was incompetent or died without a male heir.

Now, the British refused to recognize Damodar Rao's adoption, and decided to annex Jhansi using this doctrine. The queen was informed in February 1854 that Jhansi was being taken over due to the 'lack of a legitimate male heir'. Rani Laxmibai would be given an allowance or pension and Jhansi would be under the rule of the governor of the North-western Provinces like 'all the other British states of Bundelkhand'. Major Ellis, a British officer who was on cordial terms with the queen, was appointed administrator of Jhansi.

In March 1854, Major Ellis called on the queen and read out the letter of annexation. Rani Laxmibai sat behind a screen and listened. After the letter was read out to her, Laxmibai said, furious: 'Meri Jhansi nahin doongi' (I will not give away my Jhansi).

> Lord Dalhousie, who was the governor-general of India from 1848 to 1856, introduced a policy called Doctrine of Lapse. The Doctrine of Lapse stated that if a ruler died without a 'legitimate male heir', the state would be annexed, or taken over, by the British. Some of the states annexed in this manner were Satara in 1848, followed by Jaitpur, Sambalpur, Baghat, Udaipur, Jhansi and Nagpur within the next six to seven years.

> Awadh was annexed in 1856, though the reason was different—the British alleged the ruler was 'incompetent'. The Doctrine of Lapse is seen as a ploy used by the British to get more and more states and regions in India under their control by denying Indian rulers their rights.

News soon reached the ordinary people of Jhansi, including Jhalkari and Puran. Jhalkari felt one with the queen. 'Yes, Jhansi is ours. It does not belong to the British. We will not give away our beloved Jhansi,' she told Puran.

Chapter Four

But the queen did not have a choice and had to accept the decision. The fort of Jhansi went into the possession of the British. Most soldiers were dismissed, and the people of Jhansi were all despondent. Jhalkari kept wondering what she could do to help the queen. Rani Laxmibai was all alone, with her adopted child, and wanted to convince the British to not take over the kingdom. It was not an easy task.

Sometimes, she would emerge from the palace, riding her horse Sarangi. Sometimes, she would be in a palanquin. She would head towards the Mahalakshmi Temple. People stood on both sides of the road to watch her, marvelling at the queen's beauty and valour.

Rani Laxmibai hoped she could free Jhansi through her devotion and prayers. She fed the poor and freely gave away money, food and clothes to the needy. She considered herself the guardian of the people of Jhansi and felt responsible for their well-being.

Puran had told Jhalkari stories of how Rani Laxmibai knew sword-fighting. She rode horses and practised jumping over wide ditches. She could shoot arrows and firearms. Jhalkari was in awe of her. What a brave warrior! How fit and strong! Though she was so young and had lost her husband suddenly, she had taken on the responsibility of the kingdom on her shoulders.

That year on Shivaratri—the Hindu festival celebrated in honour of Lord Shiva—Puran told Jhalkari that he had a surprise for her. Jhalkari wondered what it could be. 'Will he give me some gifts? But I don't need anything. Will he take me to the top of the hill again? That would be fun!' she thought. But it didn't appear possible on Shivaratri day, when people all over town were busy with fasting and prayers.

Puran asked Jhalkari to get dressed. 'Wear a nice saree. We are going somewhere special,' he said. Jhalkari's heart skipped a beat. Where could he be taking her? Could it be what she thought? She couldn't believe that her wildly unrealistic dreams could be coming true.

As Jhalkari stepped into the palace, she was dazzled. Women roamed about the town of Jhansi freely but here, inside the palace, women were everywhere! How pretty they all looked! Some attended to the queen, others walked about with their plates for puja containing flowers, incense sticks and earthen lamps. The lights from all the lamps in mirrors made the rooms dazzle even more.

And in the middle of all this sat an exquisitely beautiful woman in a white saree. She was so young! Her little boy was sitting by her side. Rani Laxmibai wore a pearl necklace along with an ivory-coloured saree over a matching choli and nagra slippers. She wore a diamond ring in her finger. She looked brave and regal and exuded power and kindness. Jhalkari was mesmerized.

The queen had invited many women to her palace. What Jhalkari loved most about the place was that despite the brightness and dazzle, there was a warm glow all around. She felt at home here.

The Rani knew Puran as he was in her army. As a shy Jhalkari, eyes downcast, went up to where Rani Laxmibai sat, she smiled and welcomed her. She extended her hand towards her. 'You look so much like me, Jhalkari!' she said, surprised. 'Look at that face, the arms, the eyes,' Laxmibai observed. 'If you tie your hair like me, and wear clothes like the ones that I am wearing, people will mistake you for me,' she said. 'And look at those fingers,' she said as she held Jhalkari's hands, 'I bet you can hold a rifle or sword steady and your hands won't shake a bit!'

Jhalkari left the palace that day feeling wonderful. All these years, she had been restless thinking that the British were harassing Indians in different parts of the country. But that day, after meeting the queen, she felt calm. 'We are all in safe hands,' Jhalkari told Puran. He agreed.

Over 3,000 soldiers had earlier been dismissed from Jhansi in 1854, a few months after King Gangadhar Rao had passed away. At that time, the Rani didn't have the power to deploy a proper army of soldiers. But gradually, as Jhansi became somewhat stable, she called many soldiers back. She included people from all castes, from Bundelas and Thakurs to Telis and Koris, everybody was called to join the army. She also invited the Pathans to join the army. Both Hindus and Muslims joined.

The queen got the love and support of farmers and traders alike by not pressuring them with taxes. She had ensured their prosperity by encouraging trade and various forms of arts and crafts.

Soon, Jhalkari started visiting the queen regularly. Rani Laxmibai had taken an instant liking for her. She liked Jhalkari so much that one day she asked her if she was willing to join her women's troop.

'I am planning to form a regiment of women in my army. Would you like to join it?' she asked Jhalkari. 'I know that you killed a tiger and you beat up a group of dacoits. The Jhansi army needs women like you,' she added. Jhalkari could not believe what she had just heard. 'I would love to!' she said.

The queen liked brave women like herself. Along with Jhalkari there were women like Kashi, Sundar, Mandar, Heera and others who were close aides of the queen. Rani Laxmibai had great plans for Jhansi and among them was to train women and even ordinary villagers to fight for their own security. She wanted Jhansi to be unlike any other kingdom anyone had ever seen.

The queen organized festivals in her palace where she invited women from all over the city. Women of various castes visited her, and she welcomed them with open arms. There was no discrimination. She treated them all alike whether they came on foot or in palanquins, whether they wore expensive sarees or ordinary ones, wore jewellery or not. The women sat in the open courtyard of the royal palace, and the queen walked among them, attending to each one as a royal host should. She gave them gifts, sweets and flowers. Musicians sang and a festive mood filled the air.

Finally the day arrived, when Jhalkari would join Rani Laxmibai's army. It was the beginning of a new phase in her life.

Chapter Five

Jhalkari woke up early in the morning, took her bath, chanted prayers and with Puran headed straight to meet the queen and join her army. The women and men were trained in separate sections. Laxmibai herself supervised the women's training. They would stand in queues, warm up, and start with horse riding. While training, the queen would wear an angarkha over a churidar and tie a muretha, a turban, around her head. She practised horse riding by jumping over wide ditches. When it was Jhalkari's turn, she took her horse over a massive ditch in the first attempt. Everyone cheered her feat!

The women also practised stick fighting and sword fighting. They would do weightlifting and wrestling too. They also practised shooting with bows and arrows and the same cheer followed when it was Jhalkari's turn. Very soon, she had learned—like the other women—to load ammunition into the gargantuan cannons of the Jhansi fort.

'Working in the army and training for it is very hard work, Jhalkari. It means lifting a lot of weight and being very strong,' said the queen. 'You must train your body so that these weights don't seem heavy and you can lift them and use them easily.'

Jhalkari listened carefully to Laxmibai's words. The queen certainly had a clear vision. She didn't think women should only cook, do housework and stay within the confines of home. 'Each one of us must be fit and strong to deal with attackers,' she said. The queen's unusual situation had made her a deft administrator, a brilliant strategist and a visionary.

Rani Laxmibai had agreed to accept a monthly allowance from the British, but soon she realized that the British were depriving her of Gangadhar Rao's other properties. They said that young Damodar could not inherit Gangadhar Rao's property until he was an adult, and the queen herself would not be eligible for it.

By then, Major Ellis was transferred and Major Erskine, who was in charge of Narmada, Sagar and Jabalpur, was given the administrative duties of Jhansi. Would things go well for Jhansi from now on?

Not really. The British soon claimed that the King of Jhansi still owed them 36,000 rupees as part of an earlier debt, and this debt would have to be repaid by the queen from her monthly allowances. Laxmibai objected vehemently, and it is believed by many that *this* demand was what eventually led to the clash between her and the British.

There were other reasons too. The fires of a great rebellion of Indian soldiers in the British army was spreading all over north India. It came to be known as the Sepoy Mutiny, or as it is called now, the First War of Independence against British colonial rule.

> In March 1857, an Indian soldier, Mangal Pandey, attacked British officers in the military garrison of Barrackpore. He was arrested and hanged to death. Then in April 1857, sepoys or Indian soldiers in Meerut rebelled and were severely punished. In May that year, the soldiers in Meerut—angry about their colleagues being punished—shot British officers and marched to Delhi. Indian sepoys in Delhi joined them and proclaimed Mughal emperor Bahadur Shah II as the ruler.
>
> This remarkable event led other Indian soldiers elsewhere in the country to join the revolt. Soon, it had spread throughout north India. Nana Saheb, the adopted son of the Maratha peshwa, joined the rebellion. The British had to fight

> hard. After they fought back in Delhi, Kanpur and Lucknow, the British forces also fought in Jhansi and Gwalior. Officially, the rebellion ended on 8 July 1859. There were massacres in Delhi, Kanpur and Jhansi, among other places. Elsewhere, there was bloodshed and the impact of British retaliation and vengeance was felt all over the country.

Around the time that the Mutiny was taking place in different parts of north India, something similar happened in Jhansi. Several British officers and their families—forty to sixty persons—were killed in June 1857.

The sepoys in Jhansi then wanted to head towards Delhi. They asked Rani Laxmibai for money and she handed over jewellery valued at one lakh rupees. This did not mean that she herself was supportive of the massacre in Jhansi or she had sent the soldiers to Delhi and Meerut to join the rebellion. However, the role of Rani Laxmibai in the Jhansi massacre has often been debated. She also sent messages to the British that Jhansi was vulnerable and needed protection from the Rajput principalities surrounding the kingdom.

After the Jhansi massacre, her situation became more and more difficult. The British sent for troops to protect Jhansi, and till the time they arrived, Rani Laxmibai was asked to govern Jhansi on behalf of the British, as per instructions of Major Erskine, who was in charge.

The women's wing of the army that Jhalkari joined was called Durga Dal. Every day, they would diligently mark coconut trees to set targets and practise shooting with firearms. They would do malkhamba, or climbing up a wooden pole, and wrestling. They were no longer coy and

tongue-tied. They became confident women ready to fight anyone.

During this entire process of training, Rani Laxmibai was impressed by Jhalkari Bai's attitude and power. 'I have an important announcement to make,' the queen said after one such gruelling session. Drenched in sweat, the women soldiers lined up to listen to their leader. Rani Laxmibai said with a twinkle in her eyes: '*You* will lead the women's troop, Jhalkari.'

Jhalkari Bai was thrilled to bits. All her dreams were coming true. The soldiers cheered for her as she folded her hands and accepted this position. 'I will not disappoint you, Baisaheba,' she promised, seeking her blessings.

The neighbouring states of Orchha and Datia were especially unfriendly towards Jhansi.

Around this time, Orchha's dewan Nathe Khan moved towards Jhansi, conquering some parts. He asked Rani Laxmibai to surrender her fort and Jhansi, offering to pay her the same amount of money the British were paying her. The cheek of Nathe Khan! Rani Laxmibai asked Major Erskine for help, but no help came her way. So she prepared to handle the crisis herself and a clash ensued in October 1857. The attack on Jhansi continued for a whole month, but Laxmibai managed well. Some Pathan and Rajput chiefs loyal to her supported her in this.

Around this time, Rani Laxmibai figured out that she was being held responsible for the massacre in Jhansi. She protested, but soon understood that the British were playing a dirty game with her using the heads of princely states against each other to gain more power.

She took a firm and difficult decision: she would stop pleading with the British. She declared herself the guardian of Jhansi, raised her flag over the Jhansi fort and took control over it.

Now the relations between the British and Laxmibai no longer had its earlier warmth and camaraderie. The latest act resulted in British army officer Hugh Rose advancing towards Jhansi with his soldiers in February-March 1858.

How would the brave queen fight this unprecedented war? What role was Jhalkari Bai destined to play in this momentous event?

Field Marshal Hugh Henry Rose, a senior British Army officer, was educated in Berlin and received military training in the Prussian military school. He served in Gibraltar, Malta and was part of the British liaison team attached to the Turkish forces in Syria handling a crisis caused by Mehemet Ali's occupation of Syria. Rose was also a liaison officer to the French commander-in-chief in Crimea when the Crimean War broke out in 1854. In India, he was put in charge of the Central Indian Field Force.

> **Hugh Rose** was among the many military officers to lead the British against the Indian rebels during the Sepoy Mutiny of 1857-59. Rose conducted some of the toughest operations, including the attack on and capture of Jhansi in April 1858.

> **Colin Campbell** was another officer leading the British forces. When news of the sepoys' rebellion reached England in July, he was appointed commander-in-chief of India. He reached Calcutta in August, and in November went to capture Lucknow. Campbell defeated Indian rebels led by Tantia Tope at Cawnpore (Kanpur) in December 1857, and returned to Lucknow in March 1858 for the final capture of the city.
>
> **Henry Lawrence** was another military officer who fought at Lucknow. He was wounded in July 1857 and died. **Sir Hugh Wheeler** was killed in the Cawnpore massacre in June 1857. **William Hodson** captured the Mughal emperor Bahadur Shah II and killed the Mughal princes. Hodson himself was later killed in Lucknow in March 1858.

And who was to fight him? A young woman around twenty years old with a child she and her husband had adopted a day before he passed away, in charge of a kingdom and its people, and who had desperately tried to prevent a war. But she was not alone. The queen had with her some very brave soldiers, and one of them was Jhalkari Bai.

Jhalkari Bai had by now trained herself as an expert warrior. Due to her outstanding power, strength and grit, she had become a favourite with the queen.

On 2 January 1858, news reached the British that the Sagar Fort, 200 kilometres from Jhansi, was in danger. The Indian sepoys were going to mutiny and Hugh Rose decided to go to Sagar to take care of things there. The fort was secured easily. Rose's next stop was Jhansi. He set out for Jhansi on 27 February. There were over 6,000

Indian soldiers and 1,500 European soldiers with him. More were there as back-up, being readied if they were required to fight in Jhansi.

From various parts of the country, rulers of independent principalities opposed the British and sought freedom from their rule. However, they were not organized amongst themselves to fight as a united force. The British took advantage of this. Apart from their enormous military strength, they had brought in their best army officers to lead the attack against Indians.

Chapter Six

The city of Jhansi and its fort were surrounded by high walls which had several turreted gates. There is a huge lake on one side of the city, with the Mahalakshmi Temple by its side.

The walls had ten entrance gates—Khanderao, Datia, Unnao, Orchha, Baragaon, Lakshmi, Sagar, Sainyar, Bhanderi and Jhirna. Each gate had a tower and enough room for soldiers to guard it. Three gates led to the fort from the cantonment where the army was stationed, and were specially protected. Other than a little portion in the west and the south, the city lay all around the fort. To the fort's south, there was a tower and a little distance from the tower was a low hillock. Unless the southern tower was taken over, it would be impossible to enter the city or the palace. The fort could be captured only after entering and capturing the city.

Inside Jhansi, cannons were being polished and prepared for the attack. There were many cannons, big and small, inside the fort and most had names like Ghanagaraj, Naldar, Garnala, Karakbijli, Bhawani Shankar, Arjun, Samudrasamhar and so on. The soldiers cleaned and polished their swords and firearms were readied.

News was pouring in every hour from the queen's secret service that the British were fast advancing towards Jhansi and meant to go for a direct attack. The wait began for the arrival of Hugh Rose and his army. The assault was expected to come from the southern side, which had thick greenery that provided enough cover to the attackers. For the soldiers in Jhansi, it was important to guard the southern tower as the entrance to the city and fort could be protected from this side. The queen's aide Ghulam Ghaus Khan was defending this side with his cannon

Ghanagaraj. Other important leaders such as Lalabhau Bakshi (with the cannon Karakbijli), Jhalkari Bai, Dewan Raghunath Singh, Jawahir Singh, Dilip Singh, Ramchandra Rao Deshmukh and so on were in charge of the other sides. Cannon balls and gunpowder were being manufactured within the fort.

The city walls were thick, the fort and other defence structures were enormous and sturdy. Jhansi was well prepared.

There were three mountain passes between Sagar and Jhansi. After capturing various forts and regions, on 21 March 1858, Hugh Rose was just outside Jhansi. Laxmibai's network of spies had learnt that Hugh Rose had decided to capture the southern gate. He had also placed teams on the hill facing the Orchha gate. This crucial information was passed on to Rani Laxmibai.

'He is waiting for another officer, Brigadier Stuart, to arrive with more forces but may attack even before he reaches,' the informer told the Rani. Her brave and devoted army officers Jhalkari Bai, Khuda Baksh Khan, Dewan Raghunath Singh, Dewan Jawahir Singh, Ghulam Ghaus Khan, Sundar, Mandar, Dost Khan, Lalabhau Bakshi, Moti Bai and Kashi Bai among others were by her side.

Rani Laxmibai paced up and down the hall wondering how her army could match up to the enormous firepower of the British. Again, she said she was against this war. 'Let us seek the help of Tantia Tope,' Rani Laxmibai finally said.

Tantia Tope was a Maratha general and follower of Nana Saheb. He was a prominent leader of the 1857 rebellion and had moved from one place to another to fight the British.

'But that will take time even if he agrees to help,' said Jhalkari. 'We must prepare to fight whether or not we get help from anyone else,' she said.

The queen realized that Jhalkari totally lacked fear, to the level of being impractical. Laxmibai didn't want a war, she wanted peace and prosperity. 'How can she get so excited about war?' the queen wondered, but she didn't say anything, not wanting to discourage her. Rani Laxmibai decided to promptly send messages to Tantia Tope, seeking his help.

Tantia Tope was one of the prominent leaders of the 1857 Sepoy Mutiny. He fought the British army in different parts of north India and was one of the most effective among the Indian generals. Born in 1814, he served under Nana Saheb, the adopted son of the Maratha peshwa. Nana Saheb himself was an important leader among the Indians in the 1857 rebellion.

Tope fought against the British in Kanpur, Jhansi and Gwalior, among others places. He valiantly organized Indian soldiers and fought guerrilla wars. In March 1858, he moved towards Jhansi to assist the queen, Laxmibai, and later fought along with her at Kalpi and Gwalior, among other places. He continued to fight and was pursued by the British, but in April 1859, he was betrayed and handed over to the British. He was then tried and executed by the British at Shivpuri.

Jhalkari Bai was right. It would take Tantia Tope time to respond. And an attack on Jhansi fort had already begun. Hugh Rose started firing at the southern tower on 23 March. Ghulam Ghaus Khan, Khuda Baksh Khan, Jhalkari, Sundar, Mandar and many others loaded the cannons and fired back in retaliation.

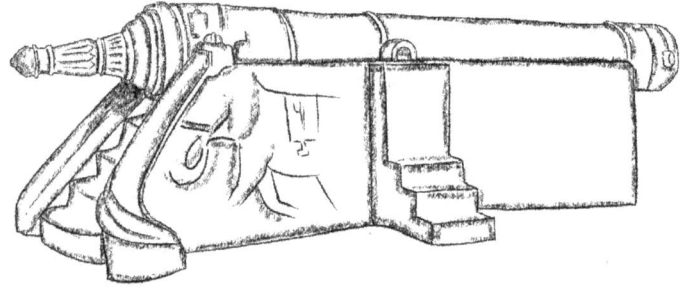

Boom! Boom! Boom! Sounds of firing and the roar of cannons reverberated through the air.

There were over 10,000 soldiers and about forty cannons inside Jhansi. Peaceful and tranquil Jhansi woke up to the pulsating sound of cannons. This was no ordinary war, it was an attack by the powerful British force on Jhansi. And how bravely the Indian soldiers fought them!

'Quick, I need to reload this gun, hand me the ammunition,' Jhalkari told Sundar. She had just spotted a group of British soldiers at a distance, loading a cannon.

Boom! The firing from Jhalkari's gun rumbled through the air. Jhalkari led the Durga Dal from the front. She was the first to fire, took quick decisions and was never afraid of consequences.

'One doesn't need to fight as retaliation. We must attack first. If we do that, the opponents will think we are confident and that we have good back-up,' that was her belief. Firing from both sides, followed by few hours of quiet, then more firing, continued for several days.

After a few days, two brave warriors who fought for Rani Laxmibai—Khuda Baksh Khan and Ghulam Ghaus Khan—were killed in the British firing. A dark cloud of hopelessness descended on Jhansi. They were their best bets, without them how long could Rani Laxmibai's army go on? Under instruction from Rani Laxmibai, they were buried inside the fort. Then Moti Bai died and she was buried there as well.

More attacks followed over the next few days. The British continued to pound the walls with cannons. A despondent queen and the soldiers were at a loss.

Hugh Rose's men were now hoping that the Jhansi side had exhausted most of their firepower and warriors. And he was right. It was then that news reached that Tantia Tope was on his way with a huge contingent of 20,000 soldiers.

Was this going to change the war?

When Hugh Rose got the same information, he used a clever strategy—to catch Tantia Tope's soldiers unawares. He divided his army and attacked Tope's soldiers from the outer flanks. This led to uncertainty and chaos as Tantia Tope's soldiers were confused and didn't know how to react. The Indian soldiers were eventually chased away and many began to flee. Over a thousand Indian soldiers were killed, but only a score of British soldiers lost their lives. Tantia Tope lost miserably because of the clever military strategy.

This was rather unexpected. Rani Laxmibai

was now becoming increasingly restless and despondent. She was in the fort with her soldiers who continued to fight all night long. The British soldiers were almost about to breach the walls now.

Meanwhile, an Indian in Jhansi acted as a British spy and agreed to open one of the gates, the Sagar Gate, for the British army. On 2 April 1858, the British soldiers were simultaneously trying to enter Jhansi through the various other gates. The Indian soldiers and even ordinary citizens tried with all their might to push the soldiers back. The attackers were shot at, pushed away and pelted with stones to prevent them from scaling the walls and breaching the gates. But once the Sagar Gate had been opened, the soldiers entered like a barrage of water into the city.

The news turned Rani Laxmibai's face ashen. From the distance, they could all see the rampage. Within a few hours, Hugh Rose's army had reached the palace. The soldiers from Laxmibai's army and the British soldiers fought a pitched battle in which they used swords and firearms. It was a direct combat. All around, there were cries of war and the sound of swords violently clashing with swords. The potent smell of gunpowder, ash and smoke filled the air.

The Indian side was overpowered easily, and the British flag was hoisted atop the palace.

Once inside the palace, Hugh Rose's soldiers looted and plundered everything inside—the mirrors were smashed and broken, precious objects were looted, books were burnt and everything lay around smashed to smithereens. The soldiers were laughing their hearts out.

What joy in destruction! What satisfaction in plunder!

According to some versions, including an account written by Vishnubhatt Godse, horrific looting and plunder followed for days and there was massacre of people in Jhansi. The murdered lay on the streets of the city.

Back in the fort on the night that the British soldiers entered Jhansi, the terrible state of affairs left Jhalkari Bai burning with anger. 'We must avenge this, Baisaheba. We must kill them all,' she raged.

The queen was shaken. The angry outburst reminded Rani Laxmibai that they needed to regroup and fight back, not give up and start lamenting.

Chapter Seven

Rani Laxmibai now called a meeting with her top soldiers. There was Ramchandra Rao Deshmukh, Jawahir Singh, Raghunath Singh, Gul Mohammed, Jhalkari, Kashi and Mandar among others.

Laxmibai initially wanted to go out and fight the British but she was dissuaded by her top officers. Most were of the opinion that Rani Laxmibai should slip away in the dark as no one had any idea how harshly she would be treated by the British. Would she be hanged? Would she be shot? Imprisoned? Tortured? No one knew for sure. But surely it would be something demeaning for the queen. Surrendering to the British was unthinkable.

Rani Laxmibai felt leaving Jhansi like that meant dishonouring her soldiers and her people.

'It doesn't mean dishonouring them. It means buying time, so you can strike back at the right opportunity,' said Jhalkari Bai. She had a plan which she wanted to share with Rani Laxmibai alone. 'With this strategy, the British army will be kept occupied and you will be able to escape,' she said.

What was her plan?

Well, the queen had often told her how curiously similar she and Jhalkari looked. Their features were the same—the same shape of the face, similar eyes, cheeks, lips and even fingers. So now it was Jhalkari Bai's turn to be the queen!

'Let me be the queen, Baisaheba,' Jhalkari pleaded with Rani Laxmibai.

Despite the crisis, Laxmibai could not help but laugh at Jhalkari's childishness. Had she lost her sanity? Why did she want to become the queen? It was no time to joke.

Jhalkari Bai paced up and down the room inside the fort, whose doors were bolted from inside. No one could hear them speak. She was bursting with excitement. Even her husband Puran had no idea of her plan. But now the time had come for her to show her skill as a fighter who could die fighting for Jhansi. It was time to save the land from the clutches of the British who had been exploiting them for years now.

'We can still turn this battle on its head with careful strategy,' she said. 'Baisaheba can move out of the fort and reorganize the army. Then she can fight back and win over Jhansi again, or it can be some other place. But she can definitely defeat the British. Only, for that, she must escape unhurt now.'

'Out with it,' commanded Rani Laxmibai. 'What is the plan?'

And so, Jhalkari Bai told the queen of her brilliant plan. And it was such a foolproof plan that there was no way Rani Laxmibai would not agree with it.

It was decided that in the darkness of the night, Rani Laxmibai would quietly slip away. She would leave Jhansi and join Tantia Tope in Kalpi and fight the British again after reestablishing a proper army and arranging adequate arms and ammunition. Jhansi was now beyond control, and unless they escaped, it would mean surrendering themselves to Hugh Rose.

Who else would go with her? Damodar Rao, Ramchandra Rao Deshmukh, Jawahir Singh, Raghunath Singh, Gul Mohammed, Kashi and Mandar. Kashi and Mandar would be dressed as men, it was decided. Along with them, there would be 400 soldiers. The road to Kalpi would be fraught with danger and the soldiers would be needed.

But before they bid adieu, it was time for Jhalkari to dress up as the Queen of Jhansi. That was her plan. She would face the British soldiers dressed as Rani Laxmibai, fooling them. They would think they were fighting the queen, whereas the real Rani Laxmibai would escape.

In the inner chambers of the Jhansi fort, Jhalkari got into a Pathan outfit—angarkha over churidar and nagra slippers. It was the queen's battle clothes. The sepia-coloured clothes were regal. Getting into them filled Jhalkari with a thrill of something momentous that was about to happen.

She carefully put a black muretha on her head over her neatly tied bun. She tied the sword with its sheath to her waist and then looked at herself in the mirror. The queen's oft-used sword, its long blade dangling from her waist, sharp and sure as herself, made her appear like Rani Laxmibai.

Jhalkari looked with uncertainty and trepidation into the mirror. The light in the chamber was grim—a reflection of the reality outside. The air was still. The suspense was killing. As soon as she looked at herself in the mirror, Jhalkari was startled. What similarity! She looked like a mirror-image of Rani Laxmibai of Jhansi. Where was Jhalkari Bai gone? Had *she* fled from one of the gates of Jhansi?

Jhalkari would give her life to protect the queen, their beloved Jhansi, her motherland. She would fight like a warrior who was not afraid to die. It was time now for Jhalkari to trick the British! She would face them and fight them, and they would think they were fighting Rani Laxmibai.

History would remember her.

She was proud of herself and of the people she represented: all those who had been thrust towards the dark corners of the world for various reasons.

Jhalkari opened the bolt of the chamber and stepped out. Passing through the various rooms of the fort, she finally reached where Rani Laxmibai was waiting. The queen was pacing up and down, tense about her forthcoming departure. As her eyes fell on the person standing in the doorway, she stopped. Laxmibai rushed towards Jhalkari Bai. 'I cannot believe my eyes!' Laxmibai said. 'Is this really you? Or is it me?'

Even in the grim situation, the two women laughed, though it was without mirth. Laxmibai embraced Jhalkari. There were tears in their eyes. She expressed gratitude to Jhalkari Bai for what she was doing for Jhansi.

'Do not thank me,' Jhalkari said. 'I am doing this out of my own gratitude to you and Jhansi.'

Though they didn't mention it, they both knew that this would be the last time they were meeting. They parted ways. The queen was on her way out of Jhansi in the murky darkness of the night with her child Damodar, other companions and 400 soldiers. Jhalkari Bai, on the other hand, was dressed as the Queen of Jhansi, and was preparing to fight the British.

Soldiers had been placed outside the boundary of Jhansi to catch Rani Laxmibai if she tried to escape. But on 4 April 1858, the queen did manage to escape along with her son Damodar and her soldiers. They divided themselves into different groups and slipped away unnoticed through the Bhanderi gate. The remaining soldiers of Jhansi divided themselves into two more groups.

Meanwhile, at the British camp, rumours were flying thick.

'Rani Laxmibai has escaped from Jhansi', 'The Rani has immolated herself', 'She is such a coward', 'Whatever may have happened, Rani Laxmibai's absence means that we have won this war'.

As the British soldiers were talking, a gallant soldier riding on a horse emerged before their eyes. The soldier, dressed like a Pathan warrior, held a shimmering sword. But wait! Was it a man or a woman?

A soldier so magnificent and formidable

could *not* be a woman, they felt. Was this an apparition? The Queen of Jhansi did have a women's wing in her army, and many of these soldiers had been fighting the British soldiers. But they could not believe that a woman warrior

could attack them out of the blue. To them, Jhansi seemed to have given up.

Was this a real soldier or the ghost of Queen Laxmibai?

'I am the Queen of Jhansi. Fight with me,' screamed Jhalkari Bai. She snapped her sword blade back and forth. The soldiers started panicking, bleeding profusely.

Jhalkari Bai instantly swerved across their path and renewed her attack vigorously. More soldiers were killed and injured. Suddenly caught unawares, there was total chaos and confoundment.

Jhalkari Bai was not alone. She was leading an able group of soldiers, women and men.

News reached Hugh Rose that Rani Laxmibai had come out of the fort and had attacked British soldiers, who were falling dead in huge numbers.

'Surround her, you fools,' yelled Rose. He was feeling rather smug about the victory after entering Jhansi, and now here was news of the queen going berserk and attacking his soldiers. 'If we catch her, it's way better than her escaping or her death,' Hugh Rose thought. 'We'll sentence her to death or kill her instantly.'

A huge number of British soldiers armed with swords and rifles surrounded Jhalkari Bai from all sides. Within a few minutes, she was forced to dismount her horse. Her sword was snatched, and her hands were tied with chains. Four British soldiers caught her and took her to Hugh Rose's camp.

A smile played on Jhalkari Bai's lips.

By then, Hugh Rose had arranged for a worker from Rani Laxmibai's palace to come and 'identify' the woman who had claimed to be the queen. After a pause of a few moments, the man whispered something into a British officer's ears, who in turn whispered something to Hugh Rose.

'Who are you?' Hugh Rose asked Jhalkari Bai.

'I am Laxmibai, the Queen of Jhansi,' Jhalkari Bai replied. 'I will not give up Jhansi, do what you have to,' she said.

Hugh Rose smirked. 'Well, you are not the queen, we already know that, don't we?'

Jhalkari Bai remained unperturbed. She knew that it was only a matter of time before her real identity was revealed. But she had done her job well. She had engaged the British soldiers in a battle followed by confusion, and the time had been utilized by the real Rani Laxmibai to melt into the dark along with other leaders and soldiers. This had gone unnoticed by the British soldiers. Soon, very soon, they would escape to Kalpi, meet up with Tantia Tope, and strike back at the British.

'If you know that I am not Rani Laxmibai, kill me. I am prepared to lay down my life for my queen, for my Jhansi and for my country,' Jhalkari Bai held her head high with pride.

Hugh Rose was impressed by the grit of this soldier. Who was she? He had no idea. But his work was done. Since this was not Rani Laxmibai, she was of no use to the British. 'Imprison her,' Rose ordered. Jhalkari Bai was taken away.

It was a strange night. Jhansi was under siege. The air was thick with smoke and the smell of burnt ammunition. Who would ensure that Jhalkari Bai remained confined in a British camp?

Seeing no one around, the brave Jhalkari Bai decided to make yet another attempt to strike at the British soldiers. She quietly slipped away from where she had been imprisoned. Now, she was ready to strike again.

Chapter Eight

Hugh Rose and his men were ready to explore Jhansi fort. There were rumours that Rani Laxmibai was dead. Some said she had escaped. But many believed that she was still in the Jhansi fort. In any case, unless the entire fort was taken over, the victory would remain incomplete. As the British officers were about to enter the fort, they saw a woman mounted on a horse, carrying a rifle, a sword hanging from her waist.

It was the same mad woman who had claimed to be Rani Laxmibai a few hours earlier! The

British officers were flabbergasted! Hadn't she been imprisoned?

A fierce battle started now between the army of Jhansi's soldiers led by Jhalkari Bai and the British soldiers. The latter was a far stronger army with more firepower, but Jhalkari Bai shone with her grit and mettle.

Her horse galloped through a sea of British militia, their red-and-white uniform like a maze ahead of her. Boom-boom! There was the constant pounding of bullets as the air quickly filled with the smell of ammunition.

Riding astride her horse, Jhalkari smiled. The blood of British and Indian soldiers had mixed together in the rubble of used shells, bullets and bodies of slain warriors. Their blood was the same red colour. Why did people not understand it?

The ear-piercing clang of swords, the boom of firearms and the screams of dying soldiers rent the air. Smoke was curling out from all over Jhansi. As Jhalkari Bai rode on her horse, with bodies of British and Indian soldiers alike lying on both sides, one of her Durga Dal soldiers called out to her from a distance, 'Puran has died fighting!' A cold shiver ran down her spine.

Ahead of her, in the distance, were troops of British infantry that she had to fight. She did not have a moment to pause and cry for her beloved husband. What a wonderful friend he had been! Jhalkari closed her eyes and said a silent prayer. 'Jhalkari Kori is so proud of Puran Kori,' she cried out. 'I will not let his sacrifice go waste.'

She quickly pulled the lead rope of the horse tied to its halter, commanding it to move faster. Up ahead, the British soldiers were on a rampage. Some were trying to enter the fort. Jhalkari decided to stop them. She swooped in on them and began a direct, forceful attack. She and her army injured several British soldiers within a few moments.

'Catch her! Or even better, kill her,' shouted a British officer. 'Don't let her cause any more damage!'

In a flash, a huge blow landed on Jhalkari Bai's chest. She felt a heavy weight knocking her down. At first, she wasn't sure what had hit her. It seemed an enormous boulder had fallen on her chest, and was weighing her down. But she didn't let go of the firearm in her grip. She kept pulling the trigger, killing or injuring those who came in the line of fire. She felt her angarkha going wet near her chest, but there was no time to check. Bit by bit, Jhalkari Bai felt her vision blurring. Perhaps she was dying? She kept shooting till the time she fell off the horse.

Jhalkari Bai fell flat on the ground. 'I hope I have been able to serve Jhansi well. I hope I have been able to serve my country well.'

Her heart stopped beating.

But her fierce spirit would never die.

Over 5,000 people were killed in Jhansi, though that figure is often debated. It is argued that the figure must have been much more.

Jhalkari Bai was able to fight many British soldiers and the time she had engaged them in fighting helped Rani Laxmibai escape to Kalpi. Soon, she would form an army again to fight the British.

Stories of Jhalkari Bai have emerged as powerful tales over the past few decades in popular Hindi Dalit literature. There are various versions in these narratives of Jhalkari Bai. Some versions say that she was killed in battle, while some stories say that she was set free and lived till 1890. Some stories say she killed a tiger as a young girl, others say that it was a wolf.

In these versions of history, Jhalkari Bai is presented as the real 'virangana' who fought without any selfish interest in riches or power. She fought only for the love of her country. These popular stories assert that while most rulers during the 1857 revolt were keen on keeping their thrones and kingdoms intact, it was actually the Dalits who had fought for the freedom of the people.

Epilogue

What happened to Rani Laxmibai after she escaped from the Jhansi fort?

When Hugh Rose found out that Rani Laxmibai had indeed escaped, he was furious and sent soldiers to chase after her. A group of British soldiers reportedly caught up with her and fought with her soldiers on Kalpi Road while she escaped along with four others, including Mandar and Kashi who were dressed as men. The queen fought face to face with an officer of the British army, whom she injured and managed to escape. Most of her soldiers were injured or killed, as she went towards Kalpi. The British officers returned to Jhansi with the wounded soldiers.

There was a massacre of the people of Jhansi as many were killed, houses were looted, plundered and set on fire. People died of hunger and thirst. Villagers were picked up and arrested. Some faced severe punishment.

The queen first reached Kalpi where she met Tantia Tope and Rao Saheb, Nana Saheb's nephew. Kalpi was about 150 kilometres from Jhansi. They collected cannons, mortar, gunpowder and a huge contingent of soldiers. Hugh Rose finally left Jhansi on 25 April after reinforcements arrived to guard the fort that they had taken.

Rani Laxmibai and Tantia Tope occupied Kalpi and prepared to defend it. On 22 May, the forces led by Rani Laxmibai were defeated by the British forces. From there, Laxmibai, Tantia Tope, the Nawab of Banda and Rao Saheb went to Gwalior, where they joined the Indian forces who were holding the city (Maharaja Scindia of Gwalior had fled to Agra). They planned to occupy the Gwalior fort, which they did quite easily. They declared Nana Saheb as their peshwa with Rao Saheb as the representative. However, other leaders from different parts of north India did not join them to fight the British.

Hugh Rose's army led another attack soon. In mid-June, Rani Laxmibai, along with an army of Indian soldiers, fought the British army. It was during this fight in June 1858 that the queen was said to have been wounded. According to some versions, she didn't want the British to capture her body and asked a hermit to cremate it. There are other versions about her death. Meanwhile, the British captured the Gwalior fort.

Today, Rani Laxmibai's tomb lies in the Phool Bagh area of Gwalior.

Jhalkari Bai
A Timeline

- 22 November 1830: Jhalkari Bai is born in Bhojla.
- 19 November 1835: Laxmibai is born in Kashi (some sources mention 1828 as the birth year).
- 20 November 1853: Gangadhar Rao, ruler of Jhansi and his wife, Rani Laxmibai, adopt a child, Ananda, and name him Damodar Gangadhar Rao.
- 21 November 1853: Gangadhar Rao dies. He was forty. Laxmibai is eighteen years old.

- February 1854: Rani Laxmibai is informed by the British that Jhansi would be annexed due to the 'lack of a legitimate male heir'.
- March 1854: British officer, Major Ellis, reads out the letter of annexation to take over Jhansi.
- March 1857: An Indian soldier, Mangal Pandey, attacks British officers in the military garrison of Barrackpore. He is arrested and hanged to death in early April.
- April 1857: Sepoys in Meerut rebel and are severely punished.
- May 1857: Indian soldiers shoot British officers in Meerut and march to Delhi. Sepoys in Delhi join them and proclaim Mughal emperor Bahadur Shah II as ruler.
- June 1857: About sixty British officers and their families are killed in Jhansi by Indian soldiers.

- 27 February 1858: British army officer Hugh Rose sets out for Jhansi to capture it from Laxmibai.
- 21 March 1858: Hugh Rose and his army reach Jhansi and prepare to attack.
- 4 April 1858, midnight: Rani Laxmibai escapes from Jhansi towards Kalpi with her son Damodar, some officers and 400 soldiers.
- 4 April 1858: Jhalkari Bai dies fighting British soldiers, pretending to be Rani Laxmibai (some stories say that she was set free and lived till 1890).
- 25 April 1858: Hugh Rose leaves Jhansi after reinforcements arrive to guard the fort.
- 22 May 1858: Rani Laxmibai and her forces are defeated by the British in Kalpi.

- 18 June 1858: Rani Laxmibai dies fighting, in Gwalior.

Author's Note

When we are taught history in school, we never wonder who wrote the textbooks and what were their sources of information. Young readers are always taught to think of history as 'authentic' and 'factual'—never to be questioned. We are not encouraged to wonder why history is so heavily tilted in favour of battles, kings, acquisition of kingdoms and riches, while there is almost nothing about the lives of the ordinary people, the poor and the women.

Is 'history' then just a record of the stories

of victorious men? Then what about 'her-story', which records the lives of women?

I feel very strongly that young readers need to know that there is perspective and politics in 'history writing'. They need to know that not just women, but Dalits, too, have been ignored in history. When it comes to Dalit women, hardly anything is known about them from the pages of history.

This is why Jhalkari Bai's story is so important. She doesn't find much space in the history of the 1857 rebellion, not even in the story of Rani Laxmibai, who is placed on a pedestal for fighting the British. Dalit writer Ramdayal Varma writes: *Yatra-tatra sarvatra milegi, unki gaatha ki charcha; kintu upekshit veervaron ka kabhi nahin chhapta parcha* (everywhere you will find discussion on their deeds, but the Dalit heroes are never written about in the papers).

So where can we find Jhalkari Bai's story? In Bhojla, where she was born. In its melas, in its songs and plays, in oral histories, and in the pages of popular Dalit literature. Her story is printed in booklets and pamphlets written in simple Hindi. They were not written by renowned historians, but by people you've never heard about. But that does not make Jhalkari Bai any less important than some of the well-known leaders who took on the British in 1857.

These books are often derided because they are not recognized or approved textbooks. Since they have not been written by trained historians, these have not found a place in mainstream history and are generally considered melodramatic and sensational.

Why are they still important? These books and the story of Jhalkari Bai draw attention to the voices of the ordinary and deprived Dalit people. In the process, they ask for their stories to be heard and acknowledged. They assert that it's time to know *their* stories too. The Dalits, who were often illiterate, did not leave behind written records but their stories are known through songs and oral narratives and there is no reason to not recognize and value them.

To write this book, I relied on Mahasweta Devi's book *The Queen of Jhansi* (published by Seagull Books, 2000) for the story of Jhansi and Rani Laxmibai, in which the author's portrayal of her is a stunning mix of valour and pathos, strength and sorrow. The author mentions how she 'collected folk material', recorded oral history, and how the queen's image is built on the 'collective memory of the people of Bundelkhand'. Jhalkari is mentioned briefly in the book. For Jhalkari's story, I read popular Hindi books, as well as *Valiant Women: Defenders of the Nation*, published by Amar Chitra Katha, and watched videos telling the popular stories. Charu Gupta's essay, 'Dalit "Viranganas" and Reinvention of 1857', published in the *Economic and Political Weekly* helped me understand the politics of Dalit history surrounding Jhalkari Bai and other 'viranganas'. I also spoke to historians and government officers from Jhansi for my research.

I would like to thank my editor and friend, Sudeshna Shome Ghosh, for giving me the opportunity to write this series. Thank you Devashish Verma for the illustrations and Radhika Shenoy for the close reading.

Swati Sengupta

Printed by BoD™in Norderstedt, Germany